Simply Read the Basics, really Discover the Details!

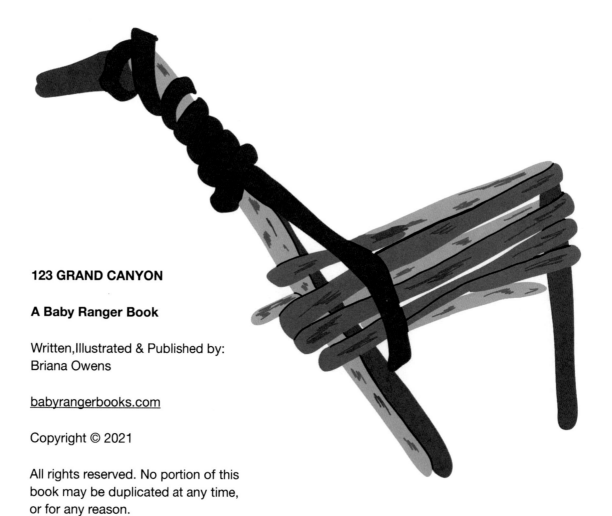

123 GRAND CANYON

A Baby Ranger Book

Written,Illustrated & Published by:
Briana Owens

babyrangerbooks.com

Copyright © 2021

Let's count together at the Grand Canyon!

1 GRAND CANYON

The canyon is 277 miles long, 18 miles wide at its widest point, and over a mile deep at the deepest spot!

Can you find Baby Ranger?

2 BASKETS

The tribal village of Supai is located in the depths of the Grand Canyon near blue-green waterfalls.

Havasuapai Basket

Havasuapai Basket

Havasupai means "people of the blue-green waters"

3 TWIG FIGURES

Twig figures like these were found in caves at the Grand Canyon.

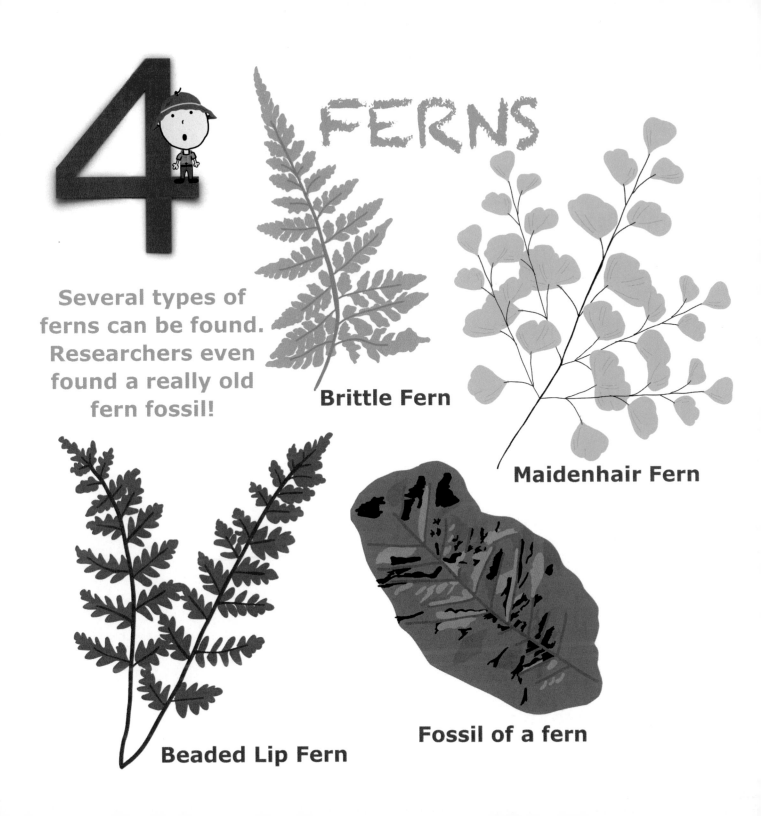

4 FERNS

Several types of ferns can be found. Researchers even found a really old fern fossil!

Brittle Fern

Maidenhair Fern

Beaded Lip Fern

Fossil of a fern

5 POTTERY PIECES

Pueblo Indians would have used pottery for carrying water or storing food.

Pueblo Miniature Olla

Tusayan Black on Red Bowl

Early Pueblo Square Designs

Pueblo Black and White Pottery

Tusayan Polychrome Bowl

Which piece of colorful old pottery is your favorite?

6 RATTLESNAKES

Speckled Rattlesnake

Hopi Rattlesnake

Prairie Rattlesnake (western)

Black-tailed Rattlesnake

Grand Canyon Pink Rattlesnake
This rattlesnake only lives at the Grand Canyon!

If you were a rattlesnake, which one would you be?

Great Basin Rattlesnake

7 SWALLOWTAILS

They look the same, but each one is a little bit different. Can you spot the differences?

Two-tailed Swallowtail

Bairds Swallowtail

Anise Swallowtail

Western Swallowtail

Kaibab Swallowtail

Desert Swallowtail

Pipevine Swallowtail

8 TREES

Six of these trees have cones. Birds and smaller animals eat the seeds from these cones.

Douglas Fir

Arizona Walnut

Colorado Blue Spruce

Englemann Spruce

Quaking Aspen

White Fir

Ponderosa Pine
This is a common tree for bats to roost in during the day.

Colorado Pinyon

Which two trees do not have cones?

9 AMPHIBIANS

Toads are bumpy and warty.
Frogs have long legs for
jumping, and salamanders
look smooth and slimy.

Red-spotted Toad

Canyon Treefrog

Arizona Tiger Salamander

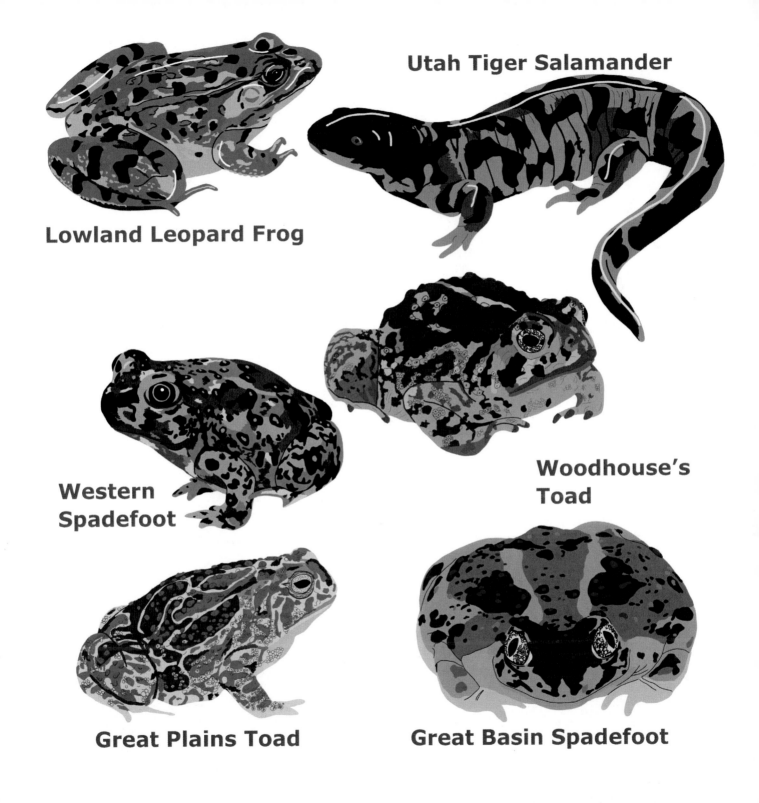

Utah Tiger Salamander

Lowland Leopard Frog

Western Spadefoot

Woodhouse's Toad

Great Plains Toad

Great Basin Spadefoot

10 NAITIVE PAINTINGS

Paintings were often created to tell stories. What stories do you think these tell?

11 MAMMALS

Remember to give wild animals space, and never feed them!

Northern Grasshopper Mouse

Rocky Mountain Elk

Black-tailed Jackrabbit

Javelina

Gunnison's Prairie Dog

Abert's Squirrel

Bighorn Sheep

Hog-nosed Skunk

Mountain Lion

Bison

Ringtail

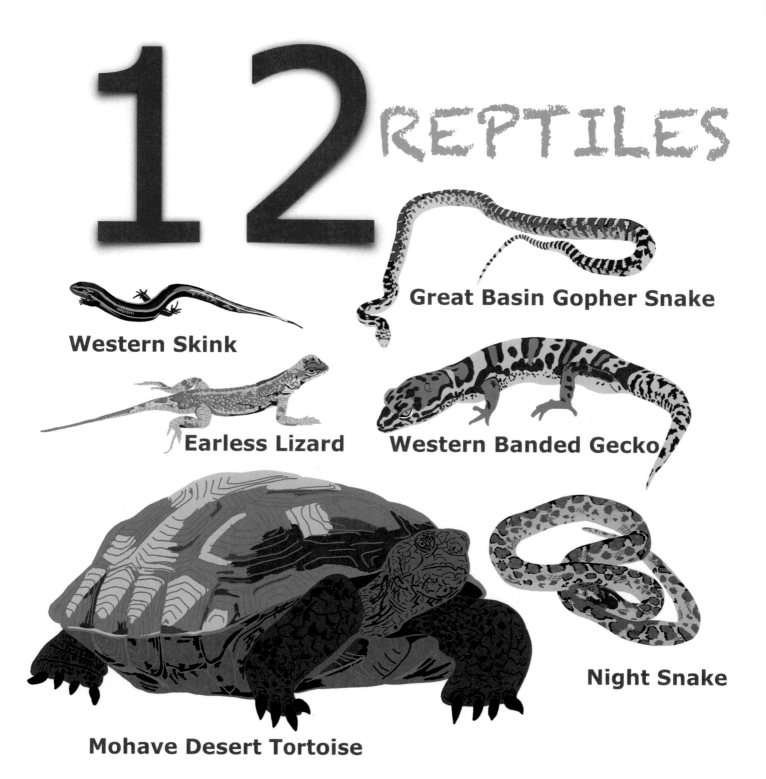

12 REPTILES

Great Basin Gopher Snake

Western Skink

Earless Lizard

Western Banded Gecko

Night Snake

Mohave Desert Tortoise

Gila Monster
(Lizard)

Western Terrestrial
Garter Snake

Sagebrush
Lizard

Sonoran
Mountain
Kingsnake

How many
lizards are
there?

Yellow-backed Spiny Lizard

Great Basin Collared Lizard

13 BIRDS

Birds of all sizes live at the Grand Canyon!

California Condor

Canyon Wren

Orchard Oriole

Greater Roadrunner

Common Merganser

American Kestrel

Indigo Bunting

Sandhill Crane

Mexican Spotted Owl

Osprey

Bald Eagle

Rufous Hummingbird

Wood Duck

14

WILDFLOWERS

Globe Mallow

Red Columbine

Blue Flax

Aster

Stream Orchid

Desert Prickly Pear

Rocky Mountain Bee Plant

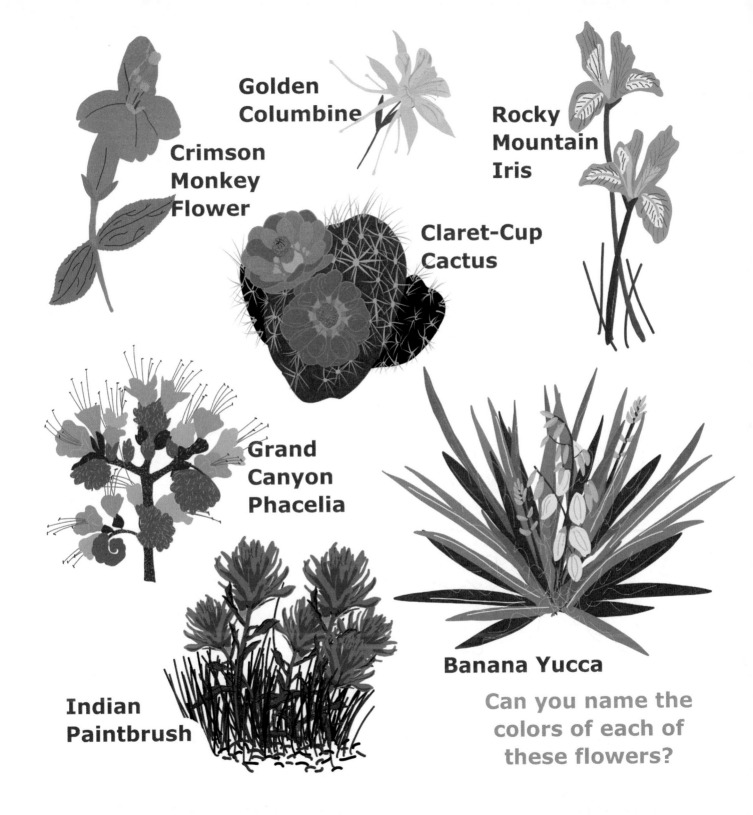

Golden Columbine

Rocky Mountain Iris

Crimson Monkey Flower

Claret-Cup Cactus

Grand Canyon Phacelia

Banana Yucca

Indian Paintbrush

Can you name the colors of each of these flowers?

15

BATS

Big Free-tailed Bat

Spotted Bat

Western Small-footed Myotis

Fringed Myotis Bat

Long-eared Myotis

Little Brown Bat

Baby Ranger Bat

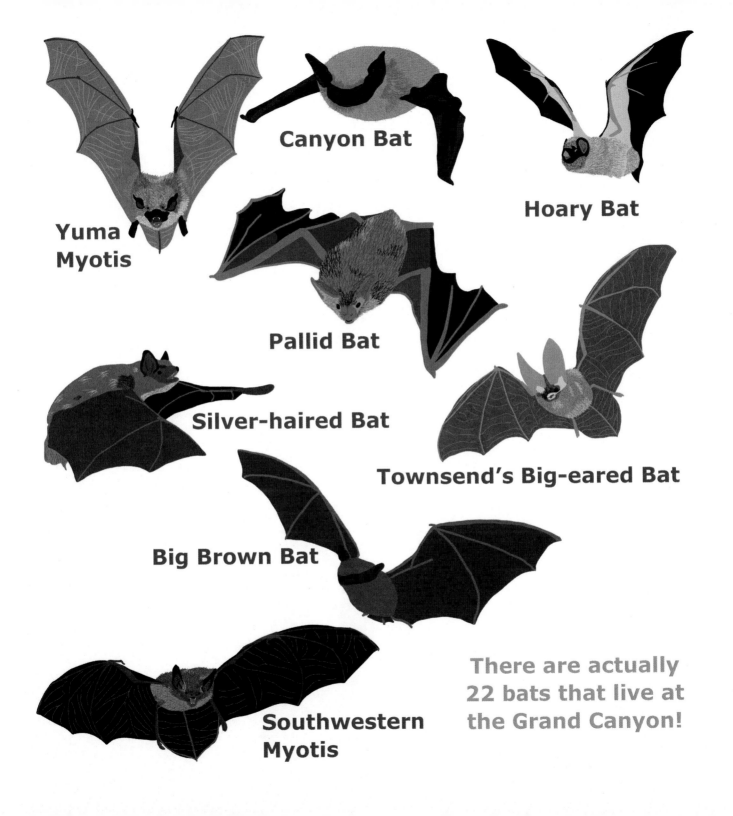

Canyon Bat

Hoary Bat

Yuma Myotis

Pallid Bat

Silver-haired Bat

Townsend's Big-eared Bat

Big Brown Bat

Southwestern Myotis

There are actually 22 bats that live at the Grand Canyon!

You counted to 15 in the GRAND CANYON!

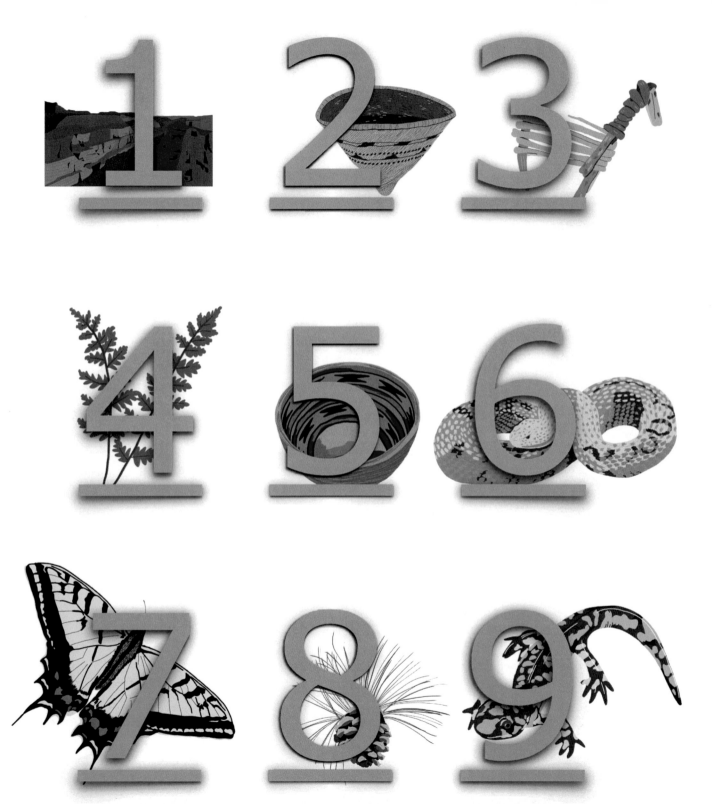

Made in the USA
Monee, IL
29 March 2022

93725093R00021